Information Report

OIG-CA-11-006

Dodd-Frank Act: Congressional Request for Information Regarding Economic Analysis by OCC

June 13, 2011

Office of Inspector General

Department of the Treasury

Contents

Appendices

Abbreviations

Dodd-Frank Act	Dodd-Frank Wall Street Reform and Consumer Protection Act
EO	Executive Order
OCC	Office of the Comptroller of the Currency
OMB	Office of Management and Budget
PRA	Paperwork Reduction Act

OIG

The Department of the Treasury
Office of Inspector General

Information Report

June 13, 2011

John G. Walsh
Acting Comptroller of the Currency

This report presents the results of our review of the economic analyses performed by the Office of the Comptroller of the Currency (OCC) related to rulemaking in order to implement the Dodd-Frank Wall Street Reform and Consumer Protection Act (P.L. 111-203) (Dodd-Frank Act). This review was conducted in response to a request for information our office received from the Ranking Member and other members of the Senate Committee on Banking, Housing, and Urban Affairs. The request letter is provided as appendix 1.

The objective of our review was to determine OCC's processes for performing economic analyses in support of rulemaking and how those processes considered the costs, benefits, and economic impact of certain proposed rules promulgated as a result of the Dodd-Frank Act.

We conducted our review in May and June 2011. In preparing our response to the request, we (1) reviewed relevant laws, executive orders (EO), and other guidance; and (2) requested, obtained and reviewed relevant information and documentation from OCC. In addition, we interviewed key OCC officials involved in the rulemaking process and related economic analyses. As recommended in the request, we limited our review of OCC's use of economic analysis in rulemaking to the following three proposed rules: (1) Credit Risk Retention, 76 FR 24090 (April 29, 2011); (2) Risk-Based Capital Standards: Advanced Capital Adequacy Framework – Basel II, Establishment of a Risk-Based Capital Floor, 75 FR 82317 (Dec. 30, 2010); and (3) Margin and Capital

Requirements for Covered Swap Entities, 76 FR 27564 (May 11, 2011).[1]

In brief, we found that OCC has processes in place to ensure that required economic analyses are performed consistently and with rigor in connection with its rulemaking authority. Furthermore, we found that those processes were followed for the three proposed rules we reviewed. We are making two recommendations in this report. Specifically, OCC should (1) develop procedures to ensure the coordination between the groups calculating administrative burden for various analyses and (2) update internal guidance to reflect the current statutory environment governing the rulemaking and related economic analysis processes, and develop related written procedures. Additionally, we noted that there was no formal process in place that provides for coordination on economic analyses between OCC and the other federal banking agencies.

Responses to Information Request

1. *Description of any statutory or other requirements to perform economic analysis.*

   The following authorities apply to OCC with regard to performing specific analyses when promulgating regulations.

   - Regulatory Flexibility Act - This act requires federal agencies to give special consideration to the impact of regulation on small businesses. The act specifies that initial and final

---

[1] The proposed rule was published after the date of the congressional request.

regulatory flexibility analyses[2] must be prepared for a regulation that will have a significant impact on a substantial number of small entities. The economic analysis that the agency prepares should incorporate the regulatory flexibility analysis, as appropriate. (5 U.S.C. § 601-12)

- Paperwork Reduction Act (PRA) - This act requires an analysis of burden to the public whenever an agency seeks to gather information from the public.[3] (44 U.S.C. § 3507(a))

- Riegle Community Development and Regulatory Improvement Act - This act requires OCC to weigh the benefits and administrative burdens of a new regulation when determining the regulation's effective date and administrative compliance requirements. (12 U.S.C. § 4802(a))

2. *Description of any internal policies, procedures, and guidance that OCC uses to ensure rigor and consistency in the economic analysis of its proposed rules.*

OCC has processes in place to ensure the rigor and consistency of economic analysis performed in connection with rulemaking. These processes were developed and in place prior to passage of the Dodd-Frank Act when the OCC was still subject to EO 12866,

---

[2] Initial and final regulatory flexibility analyses are to contain, among other things (1) a statement of the objectives of, and legal basis for, the proposed rule; (2) a description of and, where feasible, an estimate of the number of small entities to which the proposed rule will apply; and (3) a description of the projected reporting, recordkeeping and other compliance requirements of the proposed rule. An initial regulatory flexibility analysis is to also contain a description of any significant alternatives to the proposed rule which accomplish the stated objectives of applicable statutes and which minimize any significant economic impact of the proposed rule on small entities. A final regulatory flexibility analysis is to include a description of the steps the agency has taken to minimize the significant economic impact on small entities, including a statement of the factual, policy, and legal reasons for selecting the alternative adopted in the final rule and why each one of other alternatives were rejected. These analyses are not necessary if the head of the agency certifies that the rule will not, if promulgated, have a significant economic impact on a substantial number of small entities.

[3] Agencies are to establish a process to evaluate whether or not proposed collections of information should be undertaken. The process is to include (1) an evaluation of the need for the collection of information; (2) a functional description of the information to be collected; (3) a plan for the collection of the information; (4) a specific, objectively supported estimate of burden; and (5) a plan for the efficient and effective management and use of the information that is to be collected.

Regulatory Planning and Review,[4] Office of Management and Budget (OMB) Circular A-4 Regulatory Analyses, [5]and the Unfunded Mandates Reform Act of 1995.[6] The processes are designed to comply with the tenets of these governing rules as well as the Regulatory Flexibility Act and PRA.

Procedures covering the rulemaking process, as a whole, are detailed in the OCC's *Guide to Rulemaking Procedures: A Staff Manual* and *OCC Policies and Procedures Manual 1000-10: Internal OCC Review Processes for Policymaking, Rulemaking, and Other Significant Documents*. These procedures provide a framework for rule development, presentation, public comment, evaluation, and approval. They detail regulatory requirements for the performance of economic analysis in support of rulemaking and procedures governing the timing and role of the analysis in the overall development, evaluation, and approval of rules. These materials include requirements for analysis to support the determination of rule significance, the more in-depth economic analysis required for significant rulemaking, and a description of the process by which the analysis is included in rulemaking packages reviewed by OCC senior officials.

A process for the actual preparation, review, and approval of economic analysis in support of rulemaking is in place but has not been documented in a formal policies and procedures manual. In practice, economists within the OCC Policy Analysis Division work with personnel from the OCC Legislative and Regulatory Activities Division and subject matter experts elsewhere in OCC to gain an understanding of the proposed rule and its potential impacts. The

---

[4] Issued September 30, 1993, the stated objectives of this EO are to enhance planning and coordination with respect to new and existing regulations; to reaffirm the primacy of federal agencies in the regulatory decision-making process; to restore the integrity and legitimacy of regulatory review and oversight; and to make the process more accessible and open to the public. Among other things, the EO requires covered agencies to assess both the costs and the benefits of the intended regulation and, recognizing that some costs and benefits are difficult to quantify, propose or adopt a regulation only when a reasoned determination is made that the benefits of the intended regulation justify its costs.
[5] Issued September 17, 2003, Circular A-4 provides OMB's guidance to federal agencies on the development of regulatory analysis as required under EO 12866, and other related authorities.
[6] The Unfunded Mandates Reform Act of 1995, P.L. 104-4, requires Congress and federal agencies to consider the costs and benefits to state, local, and tribal governments and to the private sector before imposing federal requirements that necessitate spending by those governments or the private sector.

economists develop quantitative and qualitative measures of the potential costs and benefits of the proposed regulation. The principles of EO 12866 and OMB Circular A-4 are used as general guidance when constructing the analysis. However, the specific methodologies used may differ from rule to rule and are developed based on the economist's expertise, the data available, and an understanding of the rule and effected markets gained from collaboration with other OCC economists and legal and supervisory personnel.

As the proposed rule moves through the evaluation and approval process, the initial analysis is incrementally updated based on input from senior OCC officials and public comments. Alternatives are developed by considering realistic variations on the proposed rule and are presented in the analysis with a summary of their potential impact. A summary of the quantitative and qualitative methodologies used, critical assumptions, calculations, alternatives and results are documented in an economic analysis memorandum. This memorandum is supported with the documents, both hardcopy and electronic, used in the development of the analysis.

The Director of the OCC Policy Analysis Division is ultimately responsible for the quality of economic analysis prepared in support of rulemaking. The Director told us that prior to the submission of the economic analysis memorandum to OCC senior officials; he reviews the analysis to ensure its overall validity and quality. This review may not always be formally documented; however, it generally entails scrutiny of the methodology, assumptions, and qualitative factors along with a check of the accuracy of any calculations.

During our review, we noted two matters related to written procedures that should be addressed by OCC management.

- *OCC's Guide to OCC Rulemaking Procedures: A Staff Manual* reflects the statutory environment governing OCC rulemaking prior to the Dodd-Frank Act, which re-defined OCC as an independent regulatory agency.[7] Accordingly, the manual details procedures for compliance that are no longer applicable to OCC.

- The processes within the OCC Policy Analysis Division for preparing, documenting, and approving economic analysis related to rulemaking have not been documented in written procedures.

3. *Assessment of the degree to which relevant OCC staff understand and follow statutory and OCC's own requirements.*

    Through discussions with management and staff within the OCC Policy Analysis Division, we determined that the individuals responsible for preparing economic analysis are very much aware of and understand the statutory, regulatory, and internal requirements governing the rulemaking process and related economic analysis. This awareness has been accomplished through use of the OCC rulemaking guide, on the job training, and close collaboration between the economists performing the analysis and OCC lawyers who guide the rulemaking process. In addition, economists within the OCC Policy Analysis Division attend external training classes and conferences to keep up to date on issues for which they are responsible.

4. *Assessment of the degree to which OCC complies with these requirements.*

    Through our review of the three OCC proposed rules listed in the May 4, 2011, request for information, we determined OCC does follow statutory, regulatory, and its own internal requirements relevant to rulemaking and related economic analysis.

5. *Description of any discretionary economic analysis that OCC voluntarily undertakes on a regular or ad hoc basis in order to ensure that its rulemaking is effective and efficient.*

    An OCC official stated that OCC does not perform any discretionary economic analysis.

---

[7] Section 315 of the Dodd-Frank Act amended 44 U.S.C. § 3502(5) to designate OCC as an independent regulatory agency for purposes of Federal Information Policy.

6. *Assessment of the relevant qualifications of the staff who conduct economic analysis.*

   Economic analysis in connection with OCC rulemaking is performed by economists in the OCC Policy Analysis Division under the direction of the Director of the Policy Analysis Division. The Director holds a bachelor's degree in economics, has completed coursework for a doctorate in economics, and possesses over 30 years of experience as a financial economist. The analyses subject to our review were prepared by a Senior Financial Economist. He holds a PhD in economics and, prior to his time with OCC, he held economist positions with the Treasury Department and Federal Reserve System. We determined that the qualifications of the OCC staff responsible for economic analysis supporting its rulemaking processes are sufficient.

7. *Review of the economic analysis, if any, conducted in connection with OCC rulemaking regarding the following proposed rules: Credit Risk Retention, 76 FR 24090 (April 29, 2011); Risk-Based Capital Standards: Advanced Capital Adequacy Framework – Basel II, Establishment of a Risk-Based Capital Floor, 75 FR 82317 (Dec. 30, 2010); and Margin and Capital Requirements for Covered Swap Entities, 76 FR (April 12, 2011). The review should place particular emphasis on (a) the quantitative methodologies OCC uses to evaluate the costs and benefits of proposed rules and the effects those rules could have on job creation and economic growth; (b) the qualitative methods OCC uses to categorize or rank the effects of proposed rules; (c) the extent to which OCC considers alternative approaches to its proposed rules; (d) the extent to which OCC examines the costs, benefits, and economic impact of reasonable alternatives to its proposed rules; (e) the extent to which OCC seeks public input and expertise in evaluating the costs, benefits, and economic impact of its proposed rules, and the extent to which OCC incorporates the public input into its rule proposals; and (f) the extent the economic analysis performed by OCC with respect to its proposed rulemakings is transparent and the results reproducible.*

   We reviewed the economic analysis performed in connection with three OCC proposed rules listed in the May 4, 2011, request for information. We determined that OCC used quantitative and qualitative methodologies; considered alternatives and the impact of the alternatives; sought public input; and that OCC rulemaking was transparent and the results were generally reproducible. Specifics on these matters are detailed below.

a. **Quantitative methodologies OCC uses to evaluate the costs and benefits of proposed rules and the effects those rules could have on job creation and economic growth:** Quantitative methodologies used by OCC to determine the potential costs of proposed regulations are discussed below. It should be noted that the benefits cited for the proposed rules were generally qualitative statements.

- Credit Risk Retention, OCC:
  - Used variables from national bank Call Report[8] data that reflected possible bank securitization activity
  - Aggregated relevant data from Call Reports, and determined 208 institutions with possible bank securitization activity are national banking organizations
  - Created a formula to estimate the amount of retained risk for these national banks
  - Estimated the opportunity cost to national banks from lost lending fees and estimated administrative costs

- Risk-Based Capital Standards: Advanced Capital Adequacy Framework – Basel II, Establishment of a Risk-Based Capital Floor (referred hereafter as "Risk-Based Capital Standards"), OCC:
  - Used Call Report data to determine the number of bank holding companies that met size conditions for mandatory adoption of advanced approach rules (10 bank holding companies in total were identified)
  - Used Call Report data to estimate greatest annual impact to affected national banks at 5 percent cost of capital

---

[8] Reports of Condition and Income, referred to as Call Reports, are required by statute (12 U.S.C. § 161 for national banks) and collected by the Federal Deposit Insurance Corporation under the provision of Section 1817(a)(1) of the Federal Deposit Insurance Act. Call Report information is extensively used by the bank regulatory agencies in their daily offsite bank monitoring activities.

- <u>Margin and Capital Requirements for Covered Swap Entities</u>, OCC:
  - Used variables from Call Report Schedule RC-L, Derivatives and Off Balance Sheet Items, that reflected swap activity
  - Aggregated institutions by their top tier holding company[9]
  - Identified impacted institutions (74 impacted institutions in total were identified) using Commodity Futures Trading Commission and Securities and Exchange Commission's proposed regulatory definitions of swap dealers to determine number of banking institutions excluded from rule
  - Estimated total initial margin required for national banks ($2.05 trillion in total initial margin was estimated)

The quantitative methodologies described above were focused on quantifying costs to national banks rather than effects on job creation and economic growth. These effects were not specifically addressed.

b. **Qualitative methods OCC uses to categorize or rank the effects of proposed rules:** OCC did not use qualitative factors to determine the effects of the proposed rules as part of the economic analyses for the Credit Risk Retention and Risk-Based Capital Standards proposed rules as neither exceeded the threshold for significant regulation and therefore did not require a full cost/benefit analysis. OCC did use qualitative factors when determining the benefits for the economic analysis conducted for the Margin and Capital Requirements for Covered Swap Entities proposed rule. The factors that OCC did use were (1) ensuring the safety and soundness of the swap entity, (2) reducing the uncertainty regarding the possible exposure to swap entities, and (3) reducing the ability of firms that lack sufficient financial resources to use the swap market to take on excessive risks.

---

[9] In some cases a holding company may own another holding company which owns a national bank. So, if holding company A owned holding company B which owned a national bank, the aggregated information would be presented under holding company A. In this case, company A would be considered the bank's top tier holding company.

c. **The extent to which OCC considers alternative approaches to its proposed rules:** The Credit Risk Retention and Risk-Based Capital Standards proposed rules did not exceed significant regulation thresholds so an evaluation of alternative approaches was not required nor performed. The economic analysis for the Margin and Capital Requirements for Covered Swap Entities proposed rule included an evaluation of alternatives. These alternatives considered the impact of varying the threshold amount used to determine the swap entities that would be subject to the proposed rule and of varying the minimum transfer amount. The impact of varying the threshold amount was quantified but OCC concluded that it lacked sufficient information to quantify the effect of varying the minimum transfer amount.

d. **The extent to which OCC examines the costs, benefits, and economic impact of reasonable alternatives to its proposed rules:** As discussed in c. above, OCC was not required to evaluate alternative approaches to its proposed rules for Credit Risk Retention and Risk-Based Capital Standards. Accordingly, OCC also was not required to, and did not, assess the economic impact for these two rules. For the Margin and Capital Requirements for Covered Swap Entities proposed rule, OCC's economic analysis did include an evaluation as to the economic impact for the alternatives it considered.

e. **The extent to which OCC seeks public input and expertise in evaluating the costs, benefits, and economic impact of its proposed rules, and the extent to which OCC incorporates the public input into its rule proposals:** OCC solicited public input for the three proposed rules listed in the May 4, 2011, request for information. At the time of this review, the comment periods for the Credit Risk Retention and the Margin and Capital Requirements for Covered Swap Entities proposed rules had not ended, so OCC has not yet had the opportunity to evaluate the impact of the comments it received. The comment period for the Risk-Based Capital Standards proposed rule had been completed and, at the time of this review, OCC was in the process of evaluating comments it received.

f. **The extent to which the economic analysis performed by OCC with respect to its proposed rulemakings is transparent and the results are reproducible:** Based on our review of OCC's economic analysis of the three proposed rules listed in the May 4, 2011, request for information and discussions with OCC Policy Analysis Division personnel, we found OCC rulemaking is transparent and the results are generally reproducible. OCC personnel responsible for the PRA submission indicated that portions of the analysis are based on supervisory experience and therefore may not always be reproducible by a third party.

During our review, we noted differences between the administrative burden calculated for PRA purposes and that calculated in the economic impact analysis for the Credit Risk Retention and the Margin and Capital Requirements for Covered Swap Entities proposed rules. For the Credit Risk Retention proposed rule, the administrative burden calculated for PRA purposes was 20,483 hours while the administrative burden calculated for the impact analysis was 12,000 hours. For the Covered Swap Entities proposed rule, the PRA analysis estimated 20 entities would be impacted by the rule change while the impact analysis estimated there would be 74 entities impacted.

It should be noted that PRA analysis is required to focus on statutorily-defined "collection of information" burdens imposed on "respondents," whereas those terms are not applicable to the impact analysis, which focuses on economic costs of administrative burden on all entities subject to the rule. In this regard, the administrative burden calculated for PRA analysis is not performed by the same OCC division that prepares the economic analysis for the proposed regulation. With that in mind, we believe that the administrative burden calculations should be coordinated and, when differences exist, documented as to why.

8. *Description of any additional steps that OCC would have to take if it were subject to Executive Orders 13563 and 12866 and associated Office of Management and Budget guidance.*

If OCC was subject to EO 13563, Improving Regulation and Regulatory Review, and EO 12866, and OMB Circular A-4, it would have to submit a Notice of Proposed Regulatory Action for each rulemaking to OMB's Office of Information and Regulatory Affairs (OIRA). OCC would also have to submit all rules that it determines to be "significant regulatory actions,"[10] to OIRA for review. OCC was subject to EO 12866 prior to the Dodd-Frank Act. Accordingly, the requirements for economic analysis defined in OCC's rulemaking guide generally mirror those of EO 12866 and OMB Circular A-4. It should be noted that OCC was never subject to EO 13563[11] as that order was issued after the Dodd-Frank Act was enacted.

9. *Assessment of the extent to which OCC is considering cumulative burden of all Dodd-Frank rulemakings on market participants and the economy.*

   OCC has not performed any economic analyses as to cumulative impact of all Dodd-Frank Act rulemakings on market participants and the economy. Nevertheless, OCC officials did tell us that the question of cumulative burden has been considered and discussed. That said, OCC believes that it is effectively impossible to assess the cumulative impact at this time because no final rules have been adopted.

---

[10] EO 12866 defines "significant regulatory action" as any regulatory action that is likely to result in a rule that *may*: (1) have an annual effect on the economy of $100 million or more, or have a material adverse effect on the economy, a sector of the economy, productivity, competition, jobs, the environment, public health or safety, or State, local, or tribal governments or communities; (2) create a serious inconsistency or interfere with another agency's actions; (3) materially alter the budgetary impact of entitlements, grants, user fees, or loan programs, or the rights and obligations of recipients thereof; or (4) raise novel legal and policy issues.

[11] Issued January 18, 2011, EO 13563 supplements and reaffirms the principles, structures, and definitions governing contemporary regulatory review that were established in EO 12866. Among other things, the EO requires that regulations are to be adopted through a process that involves public participation. The EO also includes provisions for integration and innovation, flexible approaches, objectivity of any scientific and technological information and processes used to support an agency's regulatory actions, and retrospective analyses of existing rules.

Recommendations

We recommend that Comptroller of the Currency:

1. Develop procedures to ensure the coordination between the groups calculating administrative burden for various analyses and ensure that differences in results are adequately explained and that the explanation is included in OCC's rulemaking record.

2. Update the *OCC Guide to Rulemaking Procedures: A Staff Manual* to reflect the current statutory environment governing the rulemaking and related economic analysis processes, including OCC's designation as an independent regulatory agency for purposes of Federal Information Policy. Additionally, OCC's Policy Analysis Division should develop written procedures covering the preparation, documentation, and approval of economic analysis used in the rulemaking process.

Management Response

OCC concurred with our recommendations and agreed to make enhancements to OCC procedures for rulemaking, including the related economic analysis. OCC stated that new and updated written procedures would be in place by September 30, 2011.

OIG Comment

We consider OCC's planned actions to be responsive to our recommendations.

* * * * *

We appreciate the courtesies and cooperation provided to our staff during the review. If you wish to discuss the report, you may contact me at (202) 927-0384 or James Lisle, Audit Manager, at (202) 927-6345. Major contributors to this report are listed in appendix 2.

Jeffrey Dye /s/
Director of Banking Audits

Appendix 1
Request to the Inspector General of the Department of the Treasury for Information Regarding Economic Analysis by the Office of the Comptroller of the Currency

---

TIM JOHNSON, SOUTH DAKOTA, CHAIRMAN

JACK REED, RHODE ISLAND
CHARLES E. SCHUMER, NEW YORK
ROBERT MENENDEZ, NEW JERSEY
DANIEL K. AKAKA, HAWAII
SHERROD BROWN, OHIO
JON TESTER, MONTANA
HERB KOHL, WISCONSIN
MARK WARNER, VIRGINIA
JEFF MERKLEY, OREGON
MICHAEL BENNET, COLORADO
KAY HAGAN, NORTH CAROLINA

RICHARD C. SHELBY, ALABAMA
MICHAEL CRAPO, IDAHO
BOB CORKER, TENNESSEE
JIM DEMINT, SOUTH CAROLINA
DAVID VITTER, LOUISIANA
MIKE JOHANNS, NEBRASKA
PATRICK J. TOOMEY, PENNSYLVANIA
MARK KIRK, ILLINOIS
JERRY MORAN, KANSAS
ROGER F. WICKER, MISSISSIPPI

DWIGHT FETTIG, STAFF DIRECTOR
WILLIAM D. DUHNKE, REPUBLICAN STAFF DIRECTOR

United States Senate
COMMITTEE ON BANKING, HOUSING, AND
URBAN AFFAIRS
WASHINGTON, DC 20510-6075

May 4, 2011

Elizabeth A. Coleman
Inspector General
Federal Reserve Board
20th and Constitution Avenue, NW
Stop 300
Washington, D.C. 20551

H. David Kotz
Inspector General
Securities and Exchange Commission
100 F Street, NE
Washington, DC 20549

A. Roy Lavik
Inspector General
Commodity Futures Trading
Commission
Three Lafayette Centre
1155 21st Street, NW
Washington, DC 20581

The Honorable Jon T. Rymer
Inspector General
Federal Deposit Insurance Corporation
3501 N. Fairfax Drive
Arlington, VA 22226

The Honorable Eric M. Thorson
Inspector General
The Department of Treasury
1500 Pennsylvania Avenue, NW
Washington, DC 20220

Dear Inspectors General:

We write to ask each of you to initiate a review of the economic analysis performed by the regulatory agency under your supervision. Our request arises from our concern that regulatory agencies are conducting rulemakings to implement Dodd-Frank without adequately considering the costs and benefits of their rules and the effects those rules could have on the economy.

On February 15, 2011, we sent a letter to that effect to each regulatory agency.[1] We were troubled by the concerns raised by Commissioners at both the Commodity Futures Trading Commission (CFTC) and the Securities and Exchange Commission (SEC) about economic analysis at their agencies. We noted that the rules adopted under the Dodd-Frank Act will have a long-term effect on job creation and economic growth, and will affect how consumers and businesses obtain credit, allocate capital, and manage risk.

---

[1] http://crapo.senate.gov/documents/Dodd-FrankLetterFeb-11.pdf

Appendix 1
Request to the Inspector General of the Department of the Treasury for
Information Regarding Economic Analysis by the Office of the Comptroller of the
Currency

On April 15, 2011, the Office of the Inspector General for the CFTC issued an
investigative report entitled "An Investigation Regarding the Cost-Benefit Analyses
Performed by the Commodity Futures Trading Commission in Connection with
Rulemakings Undertaken Pursuant to the Dodd-Frank Act."[2] Unfortunately, the report
found a number of troubling issues with CFTC rulemaking that confirm the concerns
expressed in our February 15, 2011 letter. Here are just a few examples:

- The report found that legal formalities trumped economic analysis in the rulemaking
  process. This was exemplified by the fact that the Office of General Counsel took a
  dominant role over the Office of Chief Economist in drafting cost-benefit analyses.
  The CFTC Inspector General described this situation as "odd" for an agency that
  regularly engages in economic analysis. (Page iv.)

- The report found that CFTC staff considered economic analysis to be merely an
  administrative task, rather than a substantive part of rulemaking. The CFTC
  Inspector General discovered that team members commonly referred to the
  economic analysis as the regulation's "caboose." (Page 15.)

- The report found that the CFTC's rulemaking process does not comply with the
  President's Executive Order 'Improving Regulation and Regulatory Review.' For
  example, the CFTC Inspector General concluded that "nobody quantified internal
  costs associated with rulemaking." (Page 15.)

- The report found that CFTC staff expressed "frustration" and "confusion" about the
  difference between cost-benefit analysis and the required Paperwork Reduction Act
  statement. The CFTC Inspector General described the level of staff confusion as
  "troublesome." (Page 21.)

We are concerned that these rulemaking issues documented by the CFTC Inspector
General's Report are not unique to the CFTC and are impeding the agencies' ability to
understand the economic effects of their proposed rules. Therefore, we request that
you conduct a review of the economic analyses performed by the regulatory agency
under your supervision and prepare a written report of your findings.

Please include in your report 1) a description of any statutory or other requirements
to perform economic analysis, 2) a description of any internal policies, procedures, and
guidance that the agency uses to ensure rigor and consistency in the economic analysis
of its proposed rules, 3) an assessment of the degree to which the relevant staff of the
agency understand and follow statutory and the agency's own requirements, 4) an
assessment of the degree to which the agency complies with these requirements, 5) a
description of any discretionary economic analysis that the agency voluntarily

---

[2] http://www.cftc.gov/ucm/groups/public/@aboutcftc/documents/file/oig_investigationreport.pdf. The Office of the
Inspector General for the Commodity Futures Trading Commission undertook the investigation at the request of
Representative Frank D. Lucas, Chairman, House Committee on Agriculture, and Representative K. Michael
Conaway, Chairman, Subcommittee on General Farm Commodities and Risk.
http://agriculture.house.gov/pdf/letters/cftc_inspectorgeneral110311.pdf

Appendix 1
Request to the Inspector General of the Department of the Treasury for
Information Regarding Economic Analysis by the Office of the Comptroller of the
Currency

undertakes on a regular or *ad hoc* basis in order to ensure that its rulemaking is
effective and efficient, 6) an assessment of the relevant qualifications of the staff who
conduct economic analysis, and 7) a review of the economic analysis, if any, conducted
in connection with the agency's rulemakings, with particular emphasis on:

A. The quantitative methodologies the agency uses to evaluate the costs and benefits
of proposed rules and the effects those rules could have on job creation and
economic growth.

B. The qualitative methods the agency uses to categorize or rank the effects of
proposed rules.

C. The extent to which the agency considers alternative approaches to its proposed
rules.

D. The extent to which the agency examines the costs, benefits, and economic impact
of reasonable alternatives to its proposed rules.

E. The extent to which the agency seeks public input and expertise in evaluating the
costs, benefits, and economic impact of its proposed rules, and the extent to which
the agency incorporates the public input into its rule proposals.

F. The extent to which the economic analysis performed by the agency with respect to
its proposed rulemakings is transparent and the results are reproducible.

In light of the unprecedented number of rule proposals that have been issued since
the enactment of Dodd-Frank, we recommend that you limit your review of the agency's
use of economic analysis in rulemakings to your agency's proposed rules listed in
Attachment A. Based on your review, please make recommendations on how to
improve the rigor and consistency of the agency's economic analysis. Please also
describe any additional steps that the agency would have to take if it were subject to
Executive Orders 13563 and 12866 and associated Office of Management and Budget
(OMB) guidance.[3]

Finally, we ask that you assess the extent to which your agency is considering the
cumulative burden of all Dodd-Frank rulemakings on market participants and the
economy.

Thank you for your consideration of this request. We respectfully ask that you
respond by June 13, 2011.

---

[3] Executive Order 13563, Improving Regulation and Regulatory Review (January 18, 2011), Executive Order
12866, Regulatory Planning and Review (October 4, 1993), and OMB Circular A-4, Regulatory Analysis
(September 17, 2003) http://www.whitehouse.gov/omb/inforeg_regmatters

Appendix 1
Request to the Inspector General of the Department of the Treasury for
Information Regarding Economic Analysis by the Office of the Comptroller of the
Currency

Sincerely,

Richard Shelby

Mike Crapo

Roger Wicker

Pat Toomey

Jerry Moran

Jim DeMint

Mike Johanns

Mark Kirk

Boozman

David Vitter

Appendix 1
Request to the Inspector General of the Department of the Treasury for
Information Regarding Economic Analysis by the Office of the Comptroller of the
Currency

Attachment A
List of Rules for Review

Commodity Futures Trading Commission
1. Protection of Cleared Swaps Customer Contracts and Collateral; Conforming Amendments to the Commodity Broker Bankruptcy Provisions, April 27, 2011, 76 FR ____ (2011)
2. Risk Management Requirements for Derivatives Clearing Organizations, 76 FR 16588 (Mar. 24, 2011)
3. Swap Trading Relationship Documentation Requirements for Swap Dealers and Major Swap Participants, 76 FR 6715 (Feb. 8, 2011)
4. Core Principles and Other Requirements for Swap Execution Facilities, 76 FR 1214 (Jan. 7, 2011)

Federal Deposit Insurance Corporation
1. Credit Risk Retention, 76 FR 24090 (April 29, 2011)
2. Risk-Based Capital Standards: Advanced Capital Adequacy Framework – Basel II; Establishment of a Risk-Based Capital Floor, 75 FR 82317 (Dec. 30, 2010)
3. Margin and Capital Requirements for Covered Swap Entities, April 12, 2011, 76 FR ____ (2011)

Federal Reserve Board
1. Credit Risk Retention, 76 FR 24090 (April 29, 2011)
2. Risk-Based Capital Standards: Advanced Capital Adequacy Framework – Basel II; Establishment of a Risk-Based Capital Floor, 75 FR 82317 (Dec. 30, 2010)
3. Margin and Capital Requirements for Covered Swap Entities, April 12, 2011, 76 FR ____ (2011)
4. Regulation Z; Truth in Lending (April 19, 2011). 76 FR ___ (2011)
5. Financial Market Utilities, 76 FR 18445 (April 4, 2011)

Office of the Comptroller of the Currency
1. Credit Risk Retention, 76 FR 24090 (April 29, 2011)
2. Risk-Based Capital Standards: Advanced Capital Adequacy Framework – Basel II; Establishment of a Risk-Based Capital Floor, 75 FR 82317 (Dec. 30, 2010)
3. Margin and Capital Requirements for Covered Swap Entities, April 12, 2011, 76 FR ____ (2011)

Securities and Exchange Commission
1. Credit Risk Retention, 76 FR 24090 (April 29, 2011)
2. Clearing Agency Standards for Operation and Governance, 76 FR 14472 (March 16, 2011)
3. Registration and Regulation of Security-Based Swap Execution Facilities, 76 FR 10948 (Feb. 28, 2011)
4. Reporting by Investment Advisers to Private Funds and Certain Commodity Pool Operators and Commodity Trading Advisors on Form PF, 76 FR 8068 (Feb.11, 2011)
5. Registration of Municipal Advisors, 76 FR 824 (Jan. 6, 2011)
6. Conflict Minerals, 75 FR 80948 (Dec. 23, 2010)

MEMORANDUM

Comptroller of the Currency
Administrator of National Banks

Washington, DC 20219

To: Jeffrey Dye, Director of Banking Audits

From: John Walsh, Acting Comptroller of the Currency /s/

Date: June 10, 2011

Subject: Response to Draft Report Concerning Economic Analysis

---

We have received and reviewed your draft report titled "Congressional Request for Information Regarding Economic Analysis by OCC." The report presents the results of your review of the economic analyses performed by the Office of the Comptroller of the Currency (OCC) related to rulemaking in order to implement the Dodd-Frank Wall Street Reform and Consumer Protection Act (Dodd-Frank Act). The review was conducted in response to a request for information your office received from the Ranking Member and other members of the Senate Committee on Banking, Housing, and Urban Affairs.

The objective of your review was to determine OCC's processes for performing economic analyses in support of rulemaking and how those processes considered the costs, benefits, and economic impact of certain proposed rules promulgated as a result of the Dodd-Frank Act.

You concluded that OCC has processes in place to ensure that required economic analyses are performed consistently and with rigor in connection with its rulemaking authority. You also found that those processes were followed for the three proposed rules you reviewed. We concur with your conclusions.

You are recommending that the OCC: (1) develop procedures to ensure the coordination between the groups calculating administrative burden for various analyses; and, (2) update internal guidance to reflect the current statutory environment governing the rulemaking and related economic analysis processes, and develop related written procedures. We agree to make these enhancements to our procedures for rulemaking, including the related economic analysis. New and updated written procedures will be in place by September 30, 2011.

Thank you for the opportunity to review and comment on your draft report.

James Lisle, Audit Manager
Adelia Gonzales, Auditor
Olivia Scott, Auditor
Kathryn Bustell, Auditor
Alex Taubinger, Referencer

Department of the Treasury

Office of Strategic Planning and Performance Management
Office of Accounting and Internal Control

Office of the Comptroller of the Currency

Acting Comptroller of the Currency
Liaison Officer

Office of Management and Budget

OIG Budget Examiner

United States Senate

Chairman and Ranking Member
Committee on Banking, Housing, and Urban Affairs